This book belongs to

_____

_____

_____

MY JUNIOR HIGH SCHOOL STORY

My Full Name:

My Birthday:

Name of My School:

School Address:

School Website:

School Social Media:

School Mascot:

School Colors:

School Song(s):

My First Day of Junior High:

My Last Day of Junior High:

My Overall GPA:

Date I Started This Journal:

What do you remember about your very first day of junior high? Were you scared? Excited?

What were the biggest differences between junior high versus elementary school?

Did all of your friends from your elementary school enter junior high with you? Who among your friends moved to different schools?

What other schools merged into your junior high school?

What was your first impression of these "new" kids?

What kids from other schools did you eventually become friends with?

Did you stay friends with your elementary school friends during junior high? Why or why not?

How many total students were enrolled in your junior high school? Did you consider your school to be large or small?

Did you have a homeroom in junior high? Did it change every year? Describe what homeroom was like.

Did you have a locker or lockers during junior high? Did you keep the same one or change every year?

What classes did you take in junior high? Who were the teachers for each class?

Which junior high class was your absolute favorite? Who was your favorite teacher?

Which junior high class was your least favorite? Who was your least favorite teacher?

What were your junior high grades like? Did you have an end-of-junior-high GPA?

Did you find junior high school work to be difficult? Did you have a lot of homework or special projects?

What extracurricular activities did you participate in during junior high? Do you wish you'd participated in something that you didn't?

Did you continue any activities from elementary school into junior high? Did you drop anything?

Did you perform in any school plays, concerts or talent shows during junior high?

Were you involved in any activities unrelated to school such as church, clubs, organizations, etc. during junior high?

What was lunch time like during junior high? Did the whole school eat together or was it divided up by grade?

Who did you sit with during lunch? Did it change every year?

Did you bring your lunch from home or eat school lunch?
What were your favorite things to eat for lunch?

Were you ever tardy during junior high? Did you ever get detention?

How many days of school did you miss during junior high? Was it due to illness or something else?

Did you have any medical issues during junior high? Any injuries or surgeries?

Did you have P.E. in junior high? Did you have to wear a special uniform for gym class? What activities did you do?

Who were your very best friends throughout junior high?

Within your junior high, who were the most popular kids? Was there a school or class clown?

Who were the smartest kids in your junior high school?
Who were the most talented?

Who was the biggest trouble maker during your junior high school years? Were there any kids you tried to avoid?

Did your school have a newspaper? Is so, what was it called? Did you read it?

Were there any school dances during your junior high years? If so, did you go and with whom?

Did you have a falling out with any friends during junior high? Do you hope to reconcile with those people?

Did you get into any big fights during junior high? What were some of the biggest dramas that happened at your school during junior high?

Did your junior high school have spirit days? If so, did you participate and what did you do? Dress up? Decorate your locker?

Did you win any awards during junior high? Were you hoping to win something that you didn't?

Did you attend any of your school's sporting events during junior high? If so, which sports were your favorites?

What was the best day of junior high for you? What are your top five best memories of junior high?

What was the worst day of junior high for you? What are your top five worst memories of junior high?

Did you have any embarrassing moments during junior high? Are you still embarrassed or can you laugh about them now?

Did you have any crushes in junior high? Were you allowed to date?

What did you and your friends like to do for fun, both after school and on weekends, during junior high?

Where were the popular hangout spots for junior high students?

What were the popular clothing styles during your junior high school years? How would you describe your style during junior high?

What were your favorite pieces and brands of clothing that you wore throughout junior high?

What were your favorite stores to shop at and things to buy during junior high?

If you wore makeup during junior high, what were your favorite brands? Did your makeup differ during school hours versus outside of school?

What were the popular hair styles during junior high?
How did you wear your hair?

Did you get an allowance during junior high? If so, now much was it and did you have to do chores to earn it?

What vacations did you take during junior high? Did you go on vacations with family or friends?

What were your favorite movies that you watched during junior high? Did you go to the theatre or stream films at home?

Who were your favorite movies stars during junior high? Were there movies stars you did NOT like that everyone else did?

_____
_____
_____
_____
_____
_____
_____
_____
_____
_____
_____
_____
_____
_____
_____
_____
_____
_____
_____
_____
_____
_____

What were your favorite television shows during junior high? Who was your favorite TV star?

Were there TV shows that everyone else seemed to love that you never watched? Which popular television stars did you NOT like?

Who were your favorite musical bands and artists during junior high?

What were your top five favorite songs that were released during your junior high school years?

Did you have a favorite artist or song during junior high?
Were there any popular artists or songs that you
personally didn't like?

Did you attend any concerts during junior high? Is so, where were they and who did you go with?

Did you have a cell phone during junior high? What kind? Did you text a lot? Play games on it?

What social media sites were you active on during junior high? Which site is your current favorite?

Did you like watching YouTube videos during junior high? Is so, which channels and who were your favorite YouTubers?

Do you have your own YouTube channel? If not, do you want one?

Did you play video games at all this past school year? If so, which ones and on what platforms?

What were some of the biggest entertainment stories during your junior high school years? Any significant celebrity breakups or deaths?

What were some of the biggest news stories, both national and international, that occurred during your junior high school years?

Who were the school Principal and Vice-Principal during your junior high years? Did you ever have any personal encounters with them?

Did you know any of the office staff at your school? Did you ever go to the offices for anything during junior high?

Who was your school counselor for junior high? What did you see them for? Did you like them?

Who were the US President and Vice President during your junior high years? Did any local or state politicians visit your school?

Who was the class and/or school president during your junior high years? What about the other offices (vice-president, secretary, etc.)?

Did you participate in student government during your junior high years? Why or why not?

Were you in any clubs during junior high? Did you serve on any committees?

What time did school start every morning? Were you early, on time or late?

What did you do in the two hours immediately after school got out? Stay for activities, hang out, or go straight home?

Did you do homework immediately after getting home from school or save it for the next morning? Did you ever forget to do your homework?

Did you have to study a lot during junior high? Do you think school work is getting harder the older you get?

Who lived at home with you during your junior high school years? Did you live at the same address the whole time? Did you have any pets?

Did any of your school classmates live in your neighborhood? What about kids from other schools who you became friends with?

What was your favorite food during junior high? What was your favorite fast food restaurant? Your favorite full-service restaurant?

What were your favorite beverages during junior high?
Did you drink coffee? What was your favorite soda pop?

What were your favorite snacks, either at school or at home, during junior high? Did you prefer sweet or savory treats?

Were you allowed to eat or drink during your junior high school classes? Did you eat candy or chew gum during school?

Did you take any school field trips or overnight trips during junior high?

How did you spend Halloweens during junior high? Did you dress up? Go to any parties?

How did you spend Thanksgivings during junior high? What foods does your family always have on Thanksgiving?

How did you spend Christmases during junior high? What presents did you get? Did you have a stocking?

Did you exchange Christmas gifts with friends during junior high? If so, with whom and what did you give and receive?

How did you spend Valentine's Day during junior high?
Did you send or receive cards, flowers, or gifts?

How did you spend the Easter holidays during junior high? Did you get an Easter basket?

Did your family observe any other holidays during your junior high school years?

How did you spend your birthdays during junior high?
What gifts did you get?

How did you spend your junior high school Spring Breaks? How much time did you get off for Spring Breaks?

Did you get yearbooks during junior high? Did you pass them around to get autographs?

What are your plans for this coming summer?

What are the top five things you are most looking forward to in high school?

Are you nervous about moving on to high school? Will your junior high school friends all be moving with you to the same school?

What are the biggest lessons you learned during junior high?

What do you consider to be your greatest junior high accomplishments?

What are your biggest regrets about junior high?

Is there any one person you hurt during junior high that you wish you hadn't? Have you made amends to them?

_____

_____

_____

_____

_____

_____

_____

_____

_____

_____

_____

_____

_____

_____

_____

_____

_____

_____

_____

_____

_____

Who hurt you the most during junior high? Have you forgiven them?

If you could go back in time and give yourself advice before the first day of junior high, what would it be?

Have you given any thought about where you'd eventually like to attend college or what you'd like to do for a job someday?

Where would you like to live as an adult? Do you want to have a family?

If you have children someday, would you want them to attend your school? Why or why not?

Where do you see yourself in 10 years? In 20 years?

Are you happy that junior high is over? What will you miss most about junior high?

PHOTOS & MEMORABILIA

PHOTOS & MEMORABILIA

PHOTOS & MEMORABILIA

PHOTOS & MEMORABILIA

PHOTOS & MEMORABILIA

PHOTOS & MEMORABILIA

PHOTOS & MEMORABILIA

PHOTOS & MEMORABILIA

AUTOGRAPHS

AUTOGRAPHS

AUTOGRAPHS

AUTOGRAPHS

AUTOGRAPHS

AUTOGRAPHS

AUTOGRAPHS